THE BEST MLB
INFIELDERS
OF ALL TIME

By Alex Monnig

Published by ABDO Publishing Company, PO Box 398166, Minneapolis, MN 55439. Copyright © 2014 by Abdo Consulting Group, Inc. International copyrights reserved in all countries. No part of this book may be reproduced in any form without written permission from the publisher. SportsZone™ is a trademark and logo of ABDO Publishing Company.

Printed in the United States of America,
North Mankato, Minnesota
092013
012014

Editor: Chrös McDougall
Series Designer: Christa Schneider

Photo credits: Dave Hammond/AP Images, cover (left), 1 (left); Mark Lennihan/AP Images, cover (right), 1 (right); Bettmann/Corbis/AP Images, 7, 13; AP Images, 9, 11, 15, 17, 19, 21, 23, 27, 29, 31, 33, 35, 39; Larry Stoddard/AP Images, 25; David Fields/AP Images, 37; John Swart/ AP Images, 41; Denis Paquin/AP Images, 43; Roberto Barea/AP Images, 45; Kevin Larkin/AP Images, 47; Ed Reinke/AP Images, 49; Chris Kasson/AP Images, 51; Elise Amendola/AP Images, 53; Mark LoMoglio/ Icon SMI, 55; Nick Turchiaro/Icon SMI, 57; Rusty Kennedy/AP Images, 59; Icon SMI, 61

Library of Congress Control Number: 2013945894

Cataloging-in-Publication Data
Monnig, Alex.
  The best MLB infielders of all time / Alex Monnig.
    p. cm. -- (Major League Baseball's best ever)
  Includes bibliographical references and index.
  ISBN 978-1-62403-115-1
  1. Major League Baseball (Organization)--Juvenile literature. 2. Fielding (Baseball)--Juvenile literature. 3. Infielders (Baseball)--Juvenile literature. I. Title.
  796.357--dc23

                                                      2013945894

TABLE OF CONTENTS

INTRODUCTION

There is a reason why a double play is nicknamed "a pitcher's best friend."

Most of the time, these plays are turned by the players manning the infield. Sure-handed infielders can help their teams win not only with the bat but also with the glove. They are not afraid to get dirty. They do not hesitate to dive in front of baseballs traveling at rocket-like speeds off the bats of the best hitters in Major League Baseball (MLB). And they often have cannon-like arms that can fire the ball across the diamond in the blink of an eye. Whether it's at the plate or in the field, infielders have shown time and again that they are important pieces of the best teams.

Here are some of the best infielders in MLB history.

HONUS WAGNER

In 1936, the National Baseball Hall of Fame inducted its first class. Five players made the cut. Only one was an infielder. His name was Honus Wagner.

Wagner, who spent most of his career with the Pittsburgh Pirates, did not look like a great athlete. He had a stocky physique and awkwardly shaped legs. On first sight, Wagner hardly struck fear into his opponent's eyes. "The Flying Dutchman" quickly made his mark, though. He became one of the most dangerous hitters and base runners in baseball's early years.

Wagner was aggressive on the base paths. And he often got on base. From 1900 to 1911 he won eight National League (NL) batting titles in 12 years. And many of his hits were for extra bases.

Honus Wagner was in the first class of players inducted into the Baseball Hall of Fame.

His 252 triples were still the third most through 2013. Wagner also led the NL in doubles seven times. And he ranked tenth in stolen bases through 2013 with 723. Those batting skills helped Wagner become the first player to get his signature on Louisville Slugger's famous bats.

Wagner was a talented all-around defender as well. He became an everyday shortstop in 1903. Many baseball historians consider him the best all-around player to man that position. However, he also played more than 200 games each as an outfielder, first baseman, and third baseman.

Outfielder Ty Cobb played during the same era as Wagner. Cobb had the most votes of any player in the 1936 Hall of Fame class. However, even he said Wagner was "maybe the greatest star to ever take the diamond."

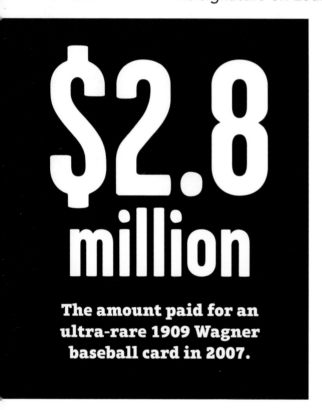

$2.8 million

The amount paid for an ultra-rare 1909 Wagner baseball card in 2007.

Honus Wagner follows through with a hit during an old timers' game in 1931.

HONUS WAGNER

Positions: Shortstop, Outfielder, First Baseman, and Third Baseman

Hometown: Chartiers, Pennsylvania

Height, Weight: 5 feet 11, 200 pounds

Birth Date: February 24, 1874

Teams: Louisville Colonels (1897–99)
Pittsburgh Pirates (1900–17)

ROGERS HORNSBY

Rogers Hornsby refused to read or watch movies for fear of damaging his hitting eye. Whatever he did, it worked. The second baseman batted better than .400 three times in his career. Those performances helped him collect three of his seven NL batting titles. He even won the Triple Crown—twice. The Triple Crown is when a hitter leads the league in batting average, home runs, and runs batted in (RBIs) in the same season.

"I don't like to sound egotistical, but every time I stepped up to the plate with a bat in my hands, I couldn't help but feel sorry for the pitcher," he said.

From 1916 to 1931, Hornsby was one of the most feared hitters in baseball. He was known for playing the game one way: at full speed.

Rogers Hornsby, shown in 1926, was one of baseball's best hitters during the early 1900s.

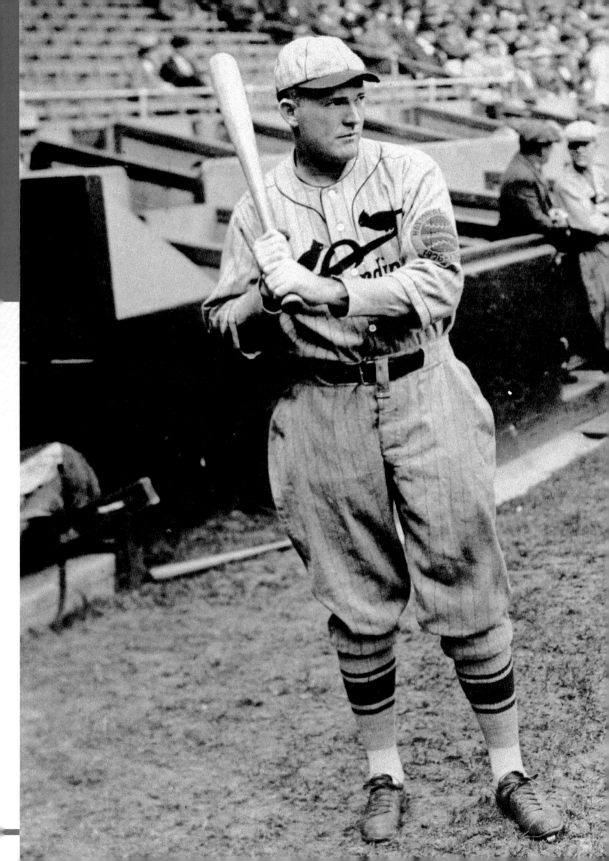

Sometimes Hornsby's personality did not make him many friends.

But he had plenty of admirers when he was in the batter's box. Hornsby twice won the NL Most Valuable Player (MVP) Award. And he finished in the top three two more times. During his career, he led the NL in every major offensive category at least once.

However, Hornsby also was an unselfish player. In 1926 he was playing for the St. Louis Cardinals. And he was having a disappointing season. Hornsby had won the NL MVP Award the previous year. But his stats dropped deeply in 1926. He had 28 fewer home runs and 50 fewer RBIs. His batting average also sunk nearly 90 points.

It was one of his worst seasons. Yet the Cardinals still won the World Series that year. Hornsby called it his "greatest moment in baseball."

.424

Hornsby's batting average in 1924—the highest since the World Series began in 1903.

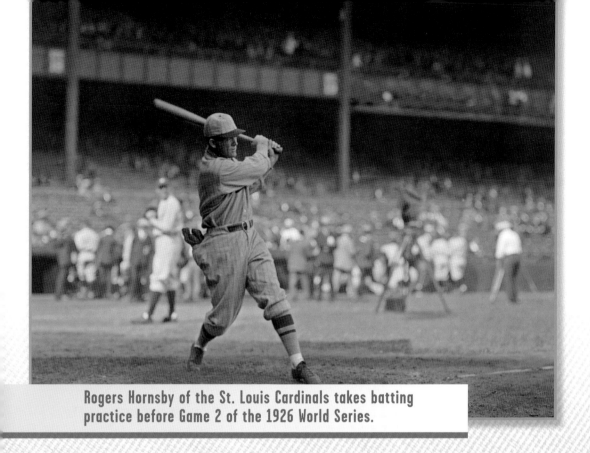

Rogers Hornsby of the St. Louis Cardinals takes batting practice before Game 2 of the 1926 World Series.

ROGERS HORNSBY

Positions: Second Baseman, Shortstop, and Third Baseman

Hometown: Winters, Texas

Height, Weight: 5 feet 11, 175 pounds

Birth Date: April 27, 1896

Teams: St. Louis Cardinals (1915–26, 1933)
New York Giants (1927),
Boston Braves (1928),
Chicago Cubs (1929–32),
St. Louis Browns (1933–37)

MVP Awards: 1925, 1929

LOU GEHRIG

Lou Gehrig stepped onto the field at Yankee Stadium on July 4, 1939. Only this time, he was not preparing to punish an opposing pitcher or man first base for the New York Yankees. He was coming to say goodbye.

A little known disease had caused Gehrig's muscles to slowly stop working. So the legendary power hitter addressed the fans at Lou Gehrig Appreciation Day.

"For the past two weeks you have been reading about the bad break I got," he said. "Yet today I consider myself the luckiest man on the face of the earth."

The fans who watched Gehrig over the years might have felt just as lucky.

Lou Gehrig, known as the "Iron Horse," played 2,130 consecutive games for the New York Yankees.

For 14 seasons as a regular, the "Iron Horse" was one of the best, most consistent players in baseball.
In fact, he played in 2,130 consecutive games. That was a record until 1995.

Gehrig's production made it easy to keep him in the lineup. His streak began in June 1925. In 1926, he began a 13-year run of scoring at least 100 runs and driving in at least 100 RBIs. His first of two American League (AL) MVP Awards came in 1927. Gehrig hit .373 with a league-leading 175 RBIs that year. He won his second MVP Award in 1936. Gehrig tied his career high with 49 home runs that season.

Gehrig was known for much of his career for partnering with teammate Babe Ruth. They were the cornerstones of the Yankees' "Murderers' Row" lineups. That group terrorized opposing pitchers in the 1920s and 1930s. And with Gehrig in the lineup, the Yankees won six World Series.

184

The number of RBIs Gehrig had in 1931—a single-season AL record that still stood in 2013.

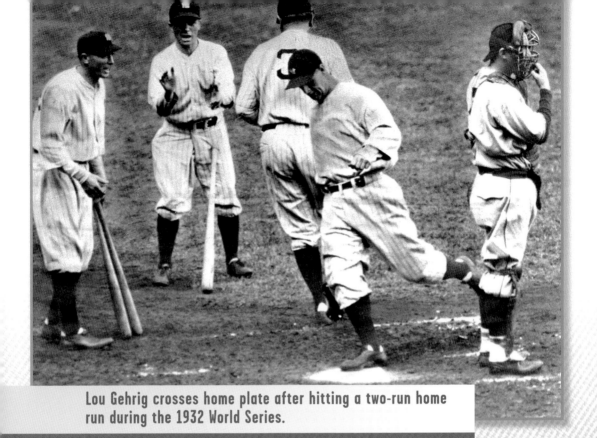

Lou Gehrig crosses home plate after hitting a two-run home run during the 1932 World Series.

LOU GEHRIG

Position: First Baseman

Hometown: New York, New York

Height, Weight: 6 feet, 200 pounds

Birth Date: June 19, 1903

Team: New York Yankees (1923–39)

All-Star Games: 1933, 1934, 1935, 1936, 1937, 1938, 1939

MVP Awards: 1927, 1936

JACKIE ROBINSON

Jackie Robinson made history when he walked out onto Ebbets Field on April 15, 1947. Baseball was the most popular sport in the United States. But until that day, MLB teams refused to sign black players. Robinson was the first. Approximately 25,000 fans were in attendance for the historic occasion.

Robinson is most famous for breaking baseball's color barrier. However, he also was a superstar athlete. Robinson had been an outstanding athlete in both high school and college. He competed in football, track, and basketball in addition to baseball. That athleticism helped him when he started playing for the Brooklyn Dodgers in 1947.

Jackie Robinson became one of MLB's top players after breaking the color barrier in 1947.

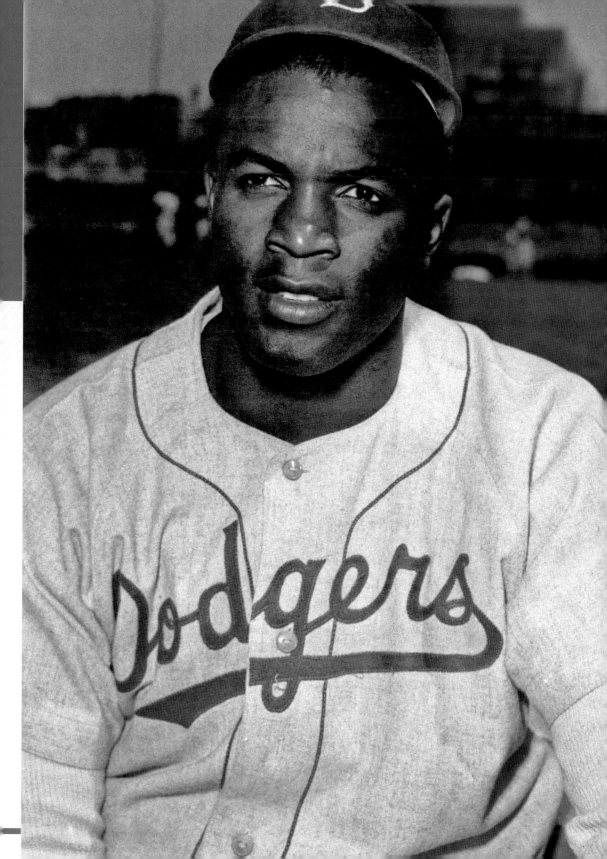

"He was the greatest competitor I've ever seen," Dodgers teammate **Duke Snider said.** "I've seen him beat a team with his bat, his ball, his glove, his feet, and, in a game in Chicago one time, with his mouth."

Fans loved Robinson's thrilling style of play. His speed stood out on the field. It helped him both on the base paths and on defense. The Dodgers played Robinson all over the field. However, he played most of his games as a second baseman. Robinson's quick hands and feet helped him lead all NL second basemen in turning double plays four seasons in a row, starting in 1949.

That year was Robinson's breakout season. He won the NL MVP Award. That season also began a stretch of six straight All-Star Game appearances. The Dodgers made it to the World Series six times in Robinson's 10 seasons, winning once.

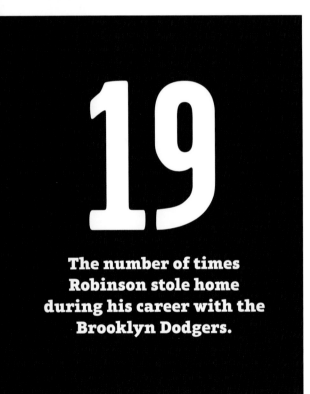

19

The number of times Robinson stole home during his career with the Brooklyn Dodgers.

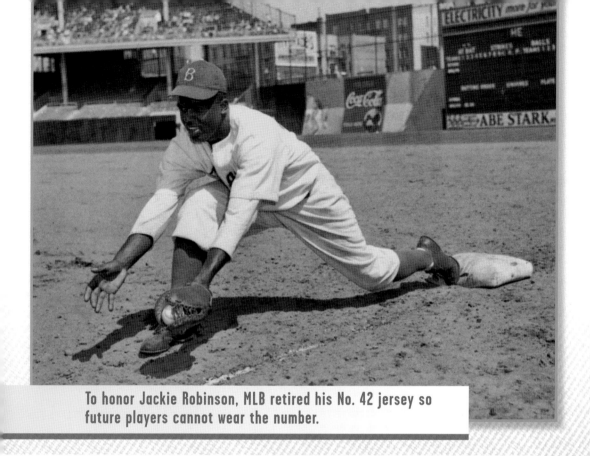

To honor Jackie Robinson, MLB retired his No. 42 jersey so future players cannot wear the number.

JACKIE ROBINSON

Positions: Second Baseman, Third Baseman, First Baseman, and Outfielder

Hometown: Cairo, Georgia

Height, Weight: 5 feet 11, 195 pounds

Birth Date: January 31, 1919

Team: Brooklyn Dodgers (1947–56)

All-Star Games: 1949, 1950, 1951, 1952, 1953, 1954

MVP Award: 1949

Rookie of the Year: 1947

ERNIE
BANKS

It was May 12, 1970. Chicago Cubs infielder Ernie Banks stepped to the plate in the second inning. He was sitting on 499 career home runs. On the third pitch, Banks sent number 500 over the ivy-covered left field wall of Wrigley Field. It was just another milestone for the man they called "Mr. Cub."

Cubs fans have had a lot of tough seasons through the years. Their team hasn't won a World Series since 1908. The bad luck has led some fans to believe the team is cursed. However, one bright spot during the team's winless century was Banks's 19 seasons on the North Side.

Ernie Banks became known as "Mr. Cub" during his 19 seasons on Chicago's North Side.

Banks was known for both smashing homers on offense and making great plays on defense. He began his major league career as a shortstop. There he led the NL in fielding percentage three times and assists twice. Banks even won a Gold Glove in 1960. Then in 1962, he moved to first base.

Banks was just as impressive at the plate. He led the NL in home runs in 1958 and 1960. He also was in the top three for homers six times. However, his two best seasons were in 1958 and 1959. Banks won the NL MVP Award in both seasons even though the Cubs finished fifth in the NL.

Banks never reached the postseason in his 19 seasons with the Cubs. However, his sunny demeanor made him a fan favorite. Banks became famous for often saying, "What a great day for baseball. Let's play two!"

47

The number of home runs Banks hit in 1958. It remained a single-season record for NL shortstops through 2013.

The Cubs' Ernie Banks follows through on a single during a 1968 game at Wrigley Field in Chicago.

ERNIE BANKS

Positions: First Baseman and Shortstop

Hometown: Dallas, Texas

Height, Weight: 6 feet 1, 180 pounds

Birth Date: January 31, 1931

Team: Chicago Cubs (1953–71)

All-Star Games: 1955, 1956, 1957, 1958, 1959, 1960, 1961, 1962, 1965, 1967, 1969

Gold Glove: 1960

MVP Awards: 1958, 1959

BROOKS
ROBINSON

Brooks Robinson was frustrating the Cincinnati Reds' hitters during the 1970 World Series. They just could not sneak a ball past him. The Baltimore Orioles' third baseman would field a ball while running into foul territory. Yet he would still throw the ball to first base for an out. Or he would dive to his side to rob the Reds of a hit.

"I'm beginning to see Brooks Robinson in my sleep," Reds manager Sparky Anderson said. "If I dropped a paper plate, he'd pick it up on one hop and throw me out at first."

With Robinson's help, the Orioles won the championship in five games.

Brooks Robinson, *right*, celebrates with pitcher Mike Cuellar after the Baltimore Orioles won the 1970 World Series.

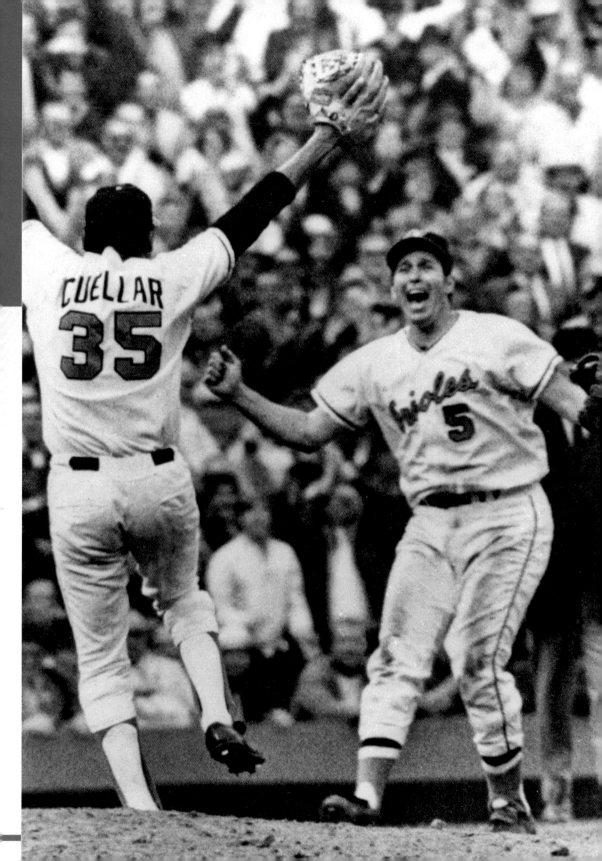

Robinson was nicknamed "the Human Vacuum Cleaner." Hardly anything got by him during his 23-year career. In fact, many agree that Robinson was the greatest fielding third baseman of all time.

Robinson was solid at the plate, too. He led the AL with 118 RBIs in 1964. However, his legend was in the field. Robinson was a career .267 hitter. He surpassed 100 RBIs just twice and never hit more than 30 home runs. Yet he appeared in the All-Star Game 15 years in a row from 1960 to 1974. He also was the 1964 AL MVP. And from 1960 to 1975, no other AL third baseman could pry the Gold Glove away from him.

"He was the best defensive player at any position," Hall of Fame teammate Frank Robinson said. "I used to stand in the outfield like a fan and watch him make play after play. I used to think 'Wow, I can't believe this.'"

15

The number of seasons in which Robinson won a Gold Glove and was selected to the All-Star Game.

Orioles third baseman Brooks Robinson makes a diving stop during a 1967 game against the New York Yankees.

BROOKS ROBINSON

Position: Third Baseman

Hometown: Little Rock, Arkansas

Height, Weight: 6 feet 1, 180 pounds

Birth Date: May 18, 1937

Team: Baltimore Orioles (1955–77)

All-Star Games: 1959, 1960, 1961, 1962, 1963, 1964, 1965, 1966, 1967, 1968, 1969, 1970, 1971, 1972, 1973, 1974

Gold Gloves: 1960, 1961, 1962, 1963, 1964, 1965, 1966, 1967, 1968, 1969, 1970, 1971, 1972, 1973, 1974, 1975

MVP Award: 1964

JOE MORGAN

The Cincinnati Reds dominated baseball in 1975 and 1976. They won the World Series both years. And they did it with a batting lineup so good that it became known as "The Big Red Machine."

All-time great hitters such as Johnny Bench and Pete Rose were in the lineup. But perhaps the most important piece of that machine was second baseman Joe Morgan.

Morgan was not known for hitting huge home runs or collecting a ton of RBIs. Rather, it was his speed and smarts that helped him become one of the best second basemen to ever take the field.

Joe Morgan follows through on a home run during the 1977 All-Star Game at Yankee Stadium in New York.

The Houston Astros traded Morgan to the Reds before the 1972 season.

It turned out to be one of the most lopsided trades of all time. Morgan had been an occasional All-Star in Houston. However, he was at his best during his eight seasons in Cincinnati. He was an All-Star in all eight seasons. And in 1975 and 1976, Morgan became the only second baseman through 2013 to win two straight MVP Awards.

Morgan starred by doing the little things. He was in the NL's top five in walks during 15 of his 22 seasons in the major leagues. He also was in the NL's top five in stolen bases 10 times and its top five in on-base percentage eight times.

Morgan was no slouch with the glove, either. He won five consecutive Gold Gloves from 1973 to 1977. His all-around contributions to the Big Red Machine helped get him elected to the Hall of Fame in 1990.

1,865

The number of walks Morgan took in his career, which ranked fifth all-time through 2013.

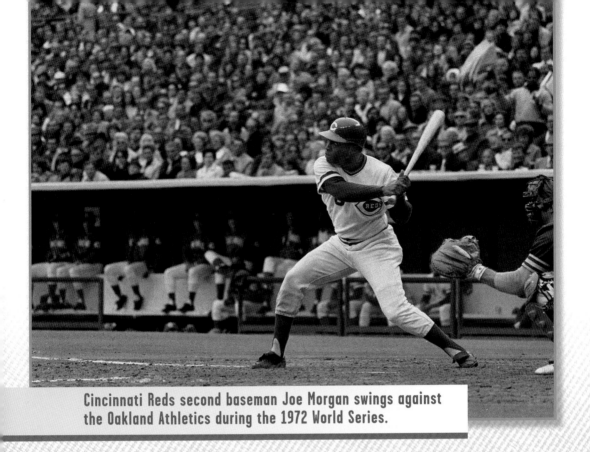

Cincinnati Reds second baseman Joe Morgan swings against the Oakland Athletics during the 1972 World Series.

JOE MORGAN

Position: Second Baseman

Hometown: Bonham, Texas

Height, Weight: 5 feet 7, 160 pounds

Birth Date: September 19, 1943

Teams: Houston Colt .45s/Astros (1963–71, 1980); Cincinnati Reds (1972–79); San Francisco Giants (1981–82); Philadelphia Phillies (1983); Oakland Athletics (1984)

All-Star Games: 1966, 1970, 1972, 1973, 1974, 1975, 1976, 1977, 1978, 1979

Gold Gloves: 1973, 1974, 1975, 1976, 1977

MVP Awards: 1975, 1976

Silver Slugger: 1982

MIKE SCHMIDT

Mike Schmidt enjoyed a breakout season in 1974. The Philadelphia Phillies' third baseman slugged an impressive 36 home runs. But it probably should have been 37.

The Phillies were on the road playing the Houston Astros that June. Schmidt clobbered a pitch and sent the ball toward the outfield seats. However, the ball struck a speaker hanging from the roof of the stadium. The speaker was approximately 117 feet (35.6 m) off the ground and 329 feet (100.3 m) away from home plate. The ball dropped into center field. And the hit was therefore ruled a single.

Schmidt became known for crushing balls like that. He led the NL in home runs eight times and finished his Hall of Fame career with 548.

Mike Schmidt starred at third base for the Philadelphia Phillies in the 1970s and 1980s.

"Schmitty" played his entire career with the Phillies. He led the team to the World Series twice, winning the title in 1980. Schmidt also won the first of his two consecutive NL MVP Awards that year. He added a third MVP Award in 1986. In all three seasons he led the league in home runs and RBIs.

What truly set Schmidt apart, however, was his defense. He was a rock at third base. Among his 10 Gold Gloves were nine in a row from 1976 to 1984.

"If you could equate the amount of time and effort put in mentally and physically into succeeding on the baseball field and measured it by the dirt on your uniform, mine would have been black," Schmidt said.

4

The number of consecutive homers Schmidt hit against the Chicago Cubs on April 17, 1976.

Mike Schmidt follows through on his 498th career home run, which he hit during a 1987 game against the New York Mets.

MIKE SCHMIDT

Position: Third Baseman

Hometown: Dayton, Ohio

Height, Weight: 6 feet 2, 195 pounds

Birth Date: September 27, 1949

Team: Philadelphia Phillies (1972–89)

All-Star Games: 1974, 1976, 1977, 1979, 1980, 1981, 1982, 1983, 1984, 1986, 1987, 1989

Gold Gloves: 1976, 1977, 1978, 1979, 1980, 1981, 1982, 1983, 1984, 1986

MVP Awards: 1980, 1981, 1986

Silver Sluggers: 1980, 1981, 1982, 1983, 1984, 1986

OZZIE SMITH

It was Game 5 of the 1985 NL Championship Series. The St. Louis Cardinals and the Los Angeles Dodgers were tied 2–2 in the bottom of the ninth inning. That is when Ozzie Smith smacked the fourth pitch he saw over the right field wall.

"Go crazy folks, go crazy!" legendary broadcaster Jack Buck famously called out. "It's a home run, and the Cardinals have won the game by the score of 3–2 on the home run by 'The Wizard!'"

It was an unlikely shot. Smith hit just 28 regular-season home runs during his 19 seasons in the big leagues. What earned him the nickname, "The Wizard," was his play at shortstop.

Ozzie Smith cheers as he rounds the bases following his game-winning home run in the 1985 NL Championship Series.

Smith began his career with the San Diego Padres. He developed into a good player during four seasons there. The Cardinals then traded for him before the 1982 season. It was there that he became a fan favorite. Before big games Smith would come onto the field with his trademark backflip. When the game started, the Wizard would dazzle crowds with his diving stops and acrobatic double-play turns. Throughout his career, he had an amazing 8,375 assists. That was the most by a shortstop and the second most by anyone through 2013.

As a hitter, Smith might have struggled to be an All-Star. As the Wizard at shortstop, however, Smith eventually became a Hall of Famer.

"I think of myself as an artist on the field," he said. "Every game I look for a chance to do something the fans have never seen before."

13

The number of Gold Gloves Smith won—more than any other shortstop through 2013.

Ozzie Smith performs his famous backflip prior to a 1987 playoff game against the San Francisco Giants.

OZZIE SMITH

Position: Shortstop

Hometown: Mobile, Alabama

Height, Weight: 5 feet 11, 150 pounds

Birth Date: December 26, 1954

Teams: San Diego Padres (1978–81),
St. Louis Cardinals (1982–96)

All-Star Games: 1981, 1982, 1983, 1984, 1985,
1986, 1987, 1988, 1989, 1990, 1991, 1992,
1994, 1995, 1996

Gold Gloves: 1980, 1981, 1982, 1983, 1984,
1985, 1986, 1987, 1988, 1989, 1990, 1991,
1992

Silver Slugger: 1987

CAL RIPKEN JR.

The Baltimore Orioles were not fighting for a playoff spot on September 6, 1995. Yet 46,804 fans—including President Bill Clinton—showed up at Camden Yards to see one man: shortstop Cal Ripken Jr.

Fifty-six years earlier, Lou Gehrig had played in his 2,130th consecutive game. It was a record thought to be untouchable. But on this night, Ripken played in his 2,131st in a row.

Ripken won the AL Rookie of the Year in his first full season in 1982. That year, he began his stretch of consecutive games. The streak lasted until September 19, 1998. Along the way, Ripken played in 2,632 straight games. He won two AL MVP Awards. And he made 19 All-Star teams. He finally retired after the 2001 season—still with the Orioles.

Cal Ripken Jr. waves to the Baltimore Orioles' home crowd in 1995 after playing in his 2,131st consecutive game.

At 6 feet 4 inches and 200 pounds, Ripken was built like a first baseman. He also hit like one. That made him unusual among shortstops. Usually they were smaller players known more for defense than hitting. But Ripken paved the way for sluggers such as Alex Rodriguez to play the demanding position as well.

Ripken also was slick in the field. He used his size to track down balls other shortstops could not reach. And he had a strong arm for throwing out runners at first base. That continued even after he moved to third base later in his career.

"I'd like to be remembered," Ripken said during his playing days. "I'd like to think that someday two guys will be talking in a bar and one of them will say something like, 'Yeah, he's a good shortstop, but he's not as good as ole Ripken was.'"

2,632

The number of consecutive games Ripken played before taking a day off on September 20, 1998.

The Baltimore Orioles' Cal Ripken Jr. fields a grounder during a 1996 game against the Kansas City Royals.

CAL RIPKEN JR.

Positions: Shortstop and Third Baseman

Hometown: Havre de Grace, Maryland

Height, Weight: 6 feet 4, 200 pounds

Birth Date: August 24, 1960

Team: Baltimore Orioles (1981–2001)

All-Star Games: 1983, 1984, 1985, 1986, 1987, 1988, 1989, 1990, 1991, 1992, 1993, 1994, 1995, 1996, 1997, 1998, 1999, 2000, 2001

Gold Gloves: 1991, 1992

MVP Awards: 1983, 1991

Rookie of the Year: 1982

Silver Sluggers: 1983, 1984, 1985, 1986, 1989, 1991, 1993, 1994

DON MATTINGLY

It was Game 2 of the 1995 AL Division Series. The New York Yankees were tied 2–2 with the Seattle Mariners. That is when Yankees first baseman Don Mattingly stepped to the plate. And with one swing, he put New York ahead with a homer to right-center field.

Mattingly had been one of the best first basemen of his generation. Yet the historically great Yankees had not made the playoffs in the first 13 years of his career. He made up for lost time, though, in the 1995 playoffs in his final season. Mattingly hit .417 with six RBIs in the five-game loss to Seattle. Mattingly's home run in Game 2 was his last in Yankee Stadium.

The New York Yankees' Don Mattingly begins his home run trot during the 1995 playoffs against the Seattle Mariners.

"Donnie Baseball" broke into the Yankees' everyday lineup as a third-year player in 1984. He led the AL with a .343 batting average and was selected for his first of six All-Star Games that season. The next season, he won the AL MVP Award while leading the league with 145 RBIs. He never led the AL in home runs. But Mattingly was a feared power source. He hit six grand slams during the 1987 season. That was a record for a single season.

There was more to Mattingly than dominant hitting, though. His .996 fielding percentage at first base placed him in the top 10 all time through 2013. He also won nine Gold Gloves. That was the most by an AL first baseman.

However, the Yankees great struggled with back problems throughout his career. Some people believe the issues were caused by Mattingly taking so many practice swings in his quest to become a great hitter.

8

The number of consecutive games in which Mattingly hit a home run in 1987, tying Dale Long's 1956 record.

Don Mattingly snags a grounder during the 1988 All-Star Game in Cincinnati.

DON MATTINGLY

Position: First Baseman

Hometown: Evansville, Indiana

Height, Weight: 6 feet, 175 pounds

Birth Date: April 20, 1961

Team: New York Yankees (1982–95)

All-Star Games: 1984, 1985, 1986, 1987, 1988, 1989

Gold Gloves: 1985 1986, 1987, 1988, 1989, 1991, 1992, 1993, 1994

MVP Award: 1985

Silver Sluggers: 1985, 1986, 1987

WADE BOGGS

The New York Yankees were down two games to one in the 1996 World Series.
It was the top of the 10th inning of Game 4. The game was still tied 6–6 with bases loaded and two outs. That's when the Yankees sent Wade Boggs in to pinch-hit.

Boggs did not chase the first pitch, trying to drive in the winning run. Instead, he did what he always did throughout his career. He showed great patience. Boggs worked the count to his favor. Finally he drew a walk. That forced in the game-winning run. New York went on to win 8–6 and later beat the Atlanta Braves in six games.

Boggs was one of the best offensive infielders of all time. But he only hit 118 home runs during his 18-year career. It was his legendary ability to get on base—either by hit or walk—that got him elected to the Hall of Fame in 2005.

Wade Boggs, shown in 1996, got on base often thanks to his batting skills and patient eye.

Some people thought Boggs's style of hitting singles and taking walks was boring to watch. But it helped his teams win games. And it helped him win five batting titles. From 1983 to 1989, Boggs went seven consecutive seasons with more than 200 hits.

And he finished in the top 10 in on-base percentage 11 times.

Boggs was not known as a great fielder early in his career. However, he won Gold Gloves late in his career in 1994 and 1995.

"I credit this award to a lot of patience and perseverance," he said of winning a Gold Glove. "With five batting titles, I wanted to prove that I could play defense and have worked hard to receive this award."

12

The number of consecutive All-Star Games Boggs was selected to from 1985 to 1996.

In 1999, Boggs reached the 3,000-hit milestone. He became the first player to do so with a home run as his 3,000th hit.

Boston Red Sox third baseman Wade Boggs whips a throw to first base during a 1986 game.

WADE BOGGS

Position: Third Baseman

Hometown: Omaha, Nebraska

Height, Weight: 6 feet 2, 190 pounds

Birth Date: June 15, 1958

Teams: Boston Red Sox (1982–92)
New York Yankees (1993–97)
Tampa Bay Devil Rays (1998–99)

All-Star Games: 1985, 1986, 1987, 1988, 1989,
1990, 1991, 1992, 1993, 1994, 1995, 1996

Gold Gloves: 1994, 1995

Silver Sluggers: 1983, 1986, 1987, 1988, 1989,
1991, 1993, 1994

ALEX RODRIGUEZ

Alex Rodriguez found himself in a home run slump in 2010. The power hitter nicknamed "A-Rod" had gone 46 at bats and 12 games without sending a ball over the wall. A slump like that was almost unheard of for the New York Yankees' third baseman. After all, he was 35 years old and had 599 home runs.

And on August 5 against the Toronto Blue Jays, the slump ended. In the first inning, Rodriguez hit a two-run shot to center field. With that, he became the youngest player to hit 600 home runs.

Rodriguez had 654 home runs through the 2013 season. That was more than any other infielder and placed him fifth all time. The all-time record is Barry Bonds's 762.

Alex Rodriguez switched from shortstop to third base when he joined the New York Yankees in 2004.

Fans had high expectations for Rodriguez from the start. The Seattle Mariners chose him first in the 1993 MLB Draft. By 1996, he was already one of the best players in the game. Cal Ripken Jr. had showed that shortstops could hit for power. Rodriguez then showed that they could hit for a lot of power. Rodriguez led the AL in home runs five times through 2013.

Rodriguez stayed in Seattle through the 2000 season. Then he signed a record 10-year, $252 million contract with the Texas Rangers. It was the largest contract in sports history. Rodriguez won the 2003 AL MVP Award. However, team success never came in Texas. Rodriguez was traded to the Yankees in 2004, and he moved to third base. He won two more MVP Awards in New York and also a World Series. However, his legacy was tainted when he admitted to using steroids from 2001 to 2003. He faced more allegations of steroid use later in his career.

24

The number of grand slams Rodriguez had hit through 2013, an MLB record.

Alex Rodriguez became a feared power hitter, but some of his stats are in question due to links to steroids.

ALEX RODRIGUEZ

Positions: Shortstop and Third Baseman

Hometown: New York, New York

Height, Weight: 6 feet 3, 225 pounds

Birth Date: July 27, 1975

Teams: Seattle Mariners (1994–2000),
Texas Rangers (2001–03),
New York Yankees (2004–)

All-Star Games: 1996, 1997, 1998, 2000, 2001,
2002, 2003, 2004, 2005, 2006, 2007, 2008,
2010, 2011

Gold Gloves: 2002, 2003

MVP Awards: 2003, 2005, 2007

Silver Sluggers: 1996, 1998, 1999, 2000, 2001,
2002, 2003, 2005, 2007, 2008

DEREK JETER

The New York Yankees' captain came up big just when his team needed him.

The "Bronx Bombers" went to Oakland for Game 3 of the 2001 AL Division Series in a 2–0 hole. The Athletics needed just one win to complete the sweep.

The Yankees held a 1–0 lead in the bottom of the seventh inning. With two outs and a runner on first, an A's batter hit a line drive to the outfield. The throw back to the infield was off target. And the A's base runner seemed certain to score. However, Jeter then appeared out of nowhere, cut it off, and tossed the ball to the catcher for the tag. New York went on to win 1–0. A few days later in Game 5, Jeter ran full-speed into the wall to catch a foul ball. He tumbled into the stands but held onto the ball for the out.

The New York Yankees' Derek Jeter hits a game-winning home run in Game 4 of the 2001 World Series.

Jeter has been coming up big for the Yankees from the beginning. He debuted in 1995, but he was Rookie of the Year and World Series champion in 1996. He helped the Yankees win four more World Series through 2013, including three in a row from 1998 to 2000.

Through 2013, Jeter was the postseason career leader in games played (158), runs scored (111), and hits (200), among other categories. In July 2011, he became only the second everyday shortstop to reach the 3,000-hit milestone. And like Wade Boggs, he did it with a home run. Jeter then went on to go 5-for-5 in the game while also driving in the winning run.

"I don't think you could script it any better," Yankees manager Joe Girardi said.

158

The record number of postseason games Jeter had played in through 2013.

Derek Jeter fields a ground ball during a 2001 game against the Philadelphia Phillies.

DEREK JETER

Position: Shortstop

Hometown: Pequannock, New Jersey

Height, Weight: 6 feet 3, 195 pounds

Birth Date: June 26, 1974

Team: New York Yankees (1995–)

All-Star Games: 1998, 1999, 2000, 2001, 2002, 2004, 2006, 2007, 2008, 2009, 2010, 2011, 2012

Gold Gloves: 2004, 2005, 2006, 2009, 2010

Rookie of the Year: 1996

Silver Sluggers: 2006, 2007, 2008, 2009, 2012

HONORABLE MENTIONS

Roberto Alomar – A slick-fielding second baseman for seven teams, Alomar was elected to 12 straight All-Star Games and won 10 Gold Gloves, mostly during the 1990s.

Rod Carew – The longtime Minnesota Twins and California Angels first and second baseman led the AL in hitting seven times and won the MVP Award in 1977 after hitting .388.

Nap Lajoie – One of the first great second basemen, Lajoie led the AL in hits four times and finished his career with 3,243 hits. He played mostly with the Cleveland Bronchos/Naps during the early 1900s.

Barry Larkin – Larkin, a Cincinnati Reds legend who played shortstop from 1986 to 2004, led the Reds to the 1990 World Series and won the 1995 NL MVP Award.

Bill Mazeroski – The Pittsburgh Pirates' second baseman was one of the greatest fielders of all time and hit a championship-winning home run in Game 7 of the 1960 World Series.

Willie McCovey – McCovey, a power-hitting first baseman who played mostly with the San Francisco Giants beginning in 1959, won the MVP Award in 1969 and bashed 521 career home runs.

Pee Wee Reese – "The Little Colonel" was a consistent presence at shortstop for the Brooklyn Dodgers teams of the 1940s and 1950s that made seven World Series appearances. He finished in the top 10 in MVP voting eight times.

Scott Rolen – Rolen excelled at the plate and at third base during his career, which was spent mostly with the Philadelphia Phillies and the St. Louis Cardinals. He won eight Gold Gloves and earned seven All-Star Game selections from 1996 through 2012.

Omar Vizquel – In addition to Ozzie Smith, Vizquel is considered one of the best fielding shortstops of all time. He played in 2,968 career games from 1989 to 2012, which was the twelfth most in history through 2013.

GLOSSARY

assists
When a defensive player throws a ball that leads to a base runner being called out.

contract
An agreement over how long a player will play for a team and how much the team will pay him.

draft
A system used by professional sports leagues to spread new talent among all of the teams.

fielding percentage
A statistic that measures a player's defense based on putouts, assists, and errors.

legend
A famous player that is remembered by fans.

on-base percentage
A statistic that measures how often a player gets on base, whether by a hit or a walk.

FOR MORE INFORMATION

Further Readings

Berman, Len. *The 25 Greatest Baseball Players of All Time.* Naperville, IL: Sourcebooks, 2010.

National Baseball Hall of Fame and Museum. *Inside the Baseball Hall of Fame.* New York: Simon & Schuster, 2013.

Ward, Geoffrey C. *Baseball: An Illustrated History.* New York: Alfred A. Knopf, 2010.

Web Links

To learn more about MLB's best infielders, visit ABDO Publishing Company online at **www.abdopublishing.com**. Web sites about MLB's best infielders are featured on our Book Links page. These links are routinely monitored and updated to provide the most current information available.

INDEX

ABOUT THE AUTHOR

Alex Monnig is a freelance journalist from St. Louis, Missouri. He graduated with his master's degree from the University of Missouri in May 2010. During his career he has spent time covering sports events around the world, including the 2008 Olympic Games in China, the 2010 Commonwealth Games in India, and the 2011 Rugby World Cup in New Zealand.